Praise for *What to Count*

"'*What counts is the circle when you dance like this*,' says Alise Alousi, letting her words echo in our minds. The distinctive voice in these poems allows the 'I' to resort to the other pronouns in reverberating at the most intimate yet public. These are poems at the service of humanity."

—Dunya Mikhail, author of *In Her Feminine Sign*

"In *What to Count*, Alise Alousi trains an unflinching eye on the life she has lived as a daughter of immigrants ('We came to Detroit for a funeral and never left / the all-electric house . . .') and as a mother and wife. But that eye is also inward looking, reliving her own dreams, that gift that, like a poem, 'turned away' as she 'slowly lifted her hand to wave.' However unrequited its gesture, that hand has never stopped waving, and these poems greet their readers with a persistent urgency. *What to Count* soars high above the fray of postindustrial America."

—Tyrone Williams, professor at SUNY Buffalo and author of *stilettos in a rifle range* (Wayne State University Press)

"*What to Count* is a lyrical arrangement of intimate vignettes, revealing the intricacies of diasporic intergenerational relations spanning multiple cultures and stages in life. The collection is divided into three sections: *Persistent* journeys of recollections unveil *Patterns* of exiled familial *Portraits*. A critical contribution to Arab and Arab American literature, marking the twentieth anniversary of the 2003 US invasion of Iraq, which began one of the longest and most demoralizing conflicts in Iraqi and American histories."

—Dena Al-Adeeb, Iraqi-born artist, writer,
educator, scholar-activist, and mother

"I've been reading and listening to Alise Alousi's poetry for a long time, captivated by both its aural and structural patterns and immediacy of experience. This is not poetry at any distance, but one feels inside a life, across the table from the poet, hearing news from a friend. There is an array of formal approaches here, as well as Alousi's commitment to her community and the care she has for it."

—Kazim Ali, author of *Sukun: New and Selected Poems*

WHAT TO COUNT

Made in Michigan Writers Series

GENERAL EDITORS

Michael Delp, Interlochen Center for the Arts
M. L. Liebler, Wayne State University

A complete listing of the books in this series can be
found online at wsupress.wayne.edu.

WHAT
TO
COUNT

Poems by Alise Alousi

WAYNE STATE UNIVERSITY PRESS
DETROIT

ISBN 9780814350706 (paperback)
ISBN 9780814350713 (e-book)

Library of Congress Control Number: 2022951519

On cover: Detail of *I see the moon and the moon sees me* by Megan Heeres, photographed by PD Rearick. Cover design by Ashley Muehlbauer.

Publication of this book was made possible by a generous gift from The Meijer Foundation.

Wayne State University Press rests on Waawiyaataanong, also referred to as Detroit, the ancestral and contemporary homeland of the Three Fires Confederacy. These sovereign lands were granted by the Ojibwe, Odawa, Potawatomi, and Wyandot nations, in 1807, through the Treaty of Detroit. Wayne State University Press affirms Indigenous sovereignty and honors all tribes with a connection to Detroit. With our Native neighbors, the press works to advance educational equity and promote a better future for the earth and all people.

Wayne State University Press
Leonard N. Simons Building
4809 Woodward Avenue
Detroit, Michigan 48201-1309

Visit us online at wsupress.wayne.edu.

In memory of my father

Majid Amin Alousi

and for my mother and siblings, always

Contents

I. Pattern

II. Persistence

III. Portrait

I

Pattern

Patterns of Departure

I thought you were going to say something else

about how the mail piled up unopened, how many
people touched the envelope, how paper

feeds grief and yet saves us. I made the font large
so you can see the words through your tears.

My eyes were bigger back then. I got sick
on planes, boats, cars, playgrounds.

I wore a favorite dress a stewardess might wear.
I was skinny and only ate cereal and consommé

and ice cream, food in bowls or something small
made in a toaster. When you opened your mouth

to speak, I never knew whether I'd hear Arabic words
or a darkness I couldn't follow. Where you started

a story wasn't always from the beginning—
a river, a woman washing clothes, a hungry man

sitting on a mat he'd woven himself, your mother
a hand on your cheek when you left home,

a yellow piece of fabric, circles of copper.
There were rumors you left behind a prison,

that you were the first in a long line, that you left
for love or left it behind, that your father was a stain

on an envelope where the stamp once was
a napkin under the table, your footprint a motif

no one wanted to wash beyond your departure.

Pandemic

Green
There's a reason his love
tastes bitter, remember the poem
where all he wanted was her want?
His boots and sword gone,
his breath a scarf of moths,
he huffs his way back home
recalls her wanting balcony,
its bleached moon, curses
the damp grass
alive beneath his feet.

Red
The red spotted insect
lands like a cough
on another one
ever-expanding
circles unloosed
in the pond.

We move like blood
spinning in test tubes
conjoined but separate
exhausted by every
pass, failed touch
your breath a thrum
in my ear.

White
There are all the numbers
left waiting in a phone,
a breathless conversation
via text, the glow
from a single white tulip
leads us to the room,
bed stripped and folded,
sorrow like dew
coating everything.
I shape his memory
into a spoon
eat from it bit by bit.

Deadline

Daniel Emmett took his inspiration from weather. Took it from another man's pen. Purported to write "Dixie" on March 31, 1859. Leaned into the breeze. Took note of clouds shifting and slowly a refrain cracked like lightning between them. Like ghosts placed this very song into his mouth, fed it to him, line by line, until his pen stopped moving and his lips started forming each simple word, and they became his own.

*　　*　　*

Or perhaps Daniel Emmett was on deadline to write a walk-around.

He was on deadline and remembered a song the African American family in his Ohio town used to sing.

He was on deadline and uninspired. He recalled. He re-called. He wrote what wasn't as his own.

The word *deadline* has its origins in the Civil War. Andersonville Prison. The deadline: wooden posts along the perimeter, a gun at the ready for those who ventured too close.

Bodies piled up near the deadline.

*　　*　　*

In that absent prison: history. In all our prisons. We lock away our stories, lock away our storied. Our storied past.

At Emanuel African Methodist Church in Charleston, South Carolina, on June 17, 1822, at midnight, 35 people were hanged for planning a slave rebellion. The original church set up in flames.

On the afternoon of June 17, 2015, there was a song, a humming no one knew. A simple whistle, a longing they thought they imagined. *Open the window and let out the noise.* Sometimes the noise is coming from right beside you.

*　　*　　*

They accepted a stranger into the circle as easy as that, pushed back their chairs. Made the space wide. Made the circle wide. Made the room wide. Wide, Why'd.

193 years to the day of the slave rebellion, nine people were massacred in Bible Study.

Clementa, Myra, Ethel Lee, Susie, Cynthia, Depayne, Sharonda, Daniel, Tywanza. A librarian. A senator. A track coach. A pastor. A pastor. A speech therapist. A student, friend, aunt, nephew, sister, brother.

*   *   *

Deadline is a printing term, a workday term, a prison term.
Black and brown bodies in fear.

Deadlines crisscross this country from Charleston to Andersonville to Baton Rouge to Walkerville. From Cleveland and Detroit to Orlando and Guantanamo.

Sometimes the noise is coming from right beside you.

Forgiveness is the smell of crushed flowers

My mother crossed the street, quickened her pace
tried to avoid the sound of him calling her name.
The flower shop on her walk home from school,
streetside windows fogged. Elaborate dresses, flounce
or lace, wasn't her thing—my grandmother
pushed her toward him, gentleman shop-owner,
a reputation, thumb on the scale.

She knew the scientific words for things he took,
to her like dance, taught her to stepwise,
stepwide through curtain, doorway, until everything
fell, face to the ground, no glimpse of sky or sun
to bend toward, just metal grates, hiss of steam heat.
She focused on the flowers enclosed in paper
or petals skimming water in white tubs,
thought, *can you lightly drown?*

Too much beauty inhaled at once lands you
somewhere like a hospital, a closet
a sofa you can't get off, like old wood floors
that creak and sway, the penny dropped
ends its run—cornered, or circling the drain.
My mother still can't walk through a door
with a bell, a shop full of flowers, without the fear
of her name, cooed or whispered.

A master gardener now, fingers curled
and stiff, the only easing of their ache,
her opening fist beneath the dirt.

Imitation Spring

Ghazal

Our daughter was born without a sense of smell in spring,
came home on the hottest day, a record-breaking spring.

At three, she pressed a fistful of lilacs to her face, inhaled hard
an imitation of what it is to smell, what I did, at the start of spring

to find flowers were color, texture only, trying embedded in her heart,
like this virus too, steals all scents, that sudden loss springing

ahead of the other symptoms; there's missing something and there's
never having it, she's old enough to know this, her eighteenth spring.

Every sense a balm and bane, hers more pronounced, that pink too
bright, hard sound of paper against itself. She lifts from a different spring.

Memory a story of want and sound, like those small figures
she gathered around her as a child, paused before the story flowered.

Now she startles us predawn, breaks her fast alone downstairs
the lunar cycle, dates and yogurt, her ode to this pandemic spring.

The condition's name we hear all year but never speak,
echoes of our late insomnia, lost lull, want of sleep.

History of Attachment

Whalebone, jet, tooth. Button owes a lot to sand against skin. When hands could no longer clutch clothing. She is powder undone and reordered, not meant to be glued. She is tricky and agile under bus seats, circling a drain or wrist, down a spine. Button runs on toes, her days at the beach meaningless. Held tight like lace, hook and eye, pedal pusher, elastic gather.

Copper is not a name she called herself. She was spent like a dime they spit shined. She loved a man that held her in his palm, things that fell open. Clamshell, toggle, grasp, grip, garter belt. The point of a collar.

Fallen, Button was useless. Stapled to a cord, hung on a door, pinned to a pillow, cardboard tucked in the corner of a mirror. Blurry from the years, not cracked or broken. Breathless at the sound of a jar screwed shut.

Password

I couldn't choose my maiden name,
first street, the month of my birth,
too close to my own breath, searchable
as the scab on my scalp I find even in sleep.
Instead: a safeword conjoined with a partner's
compound headache of consonants
interspersed with today's tally of
new illnesses, unutterable worldwide.

Not the first best dog either, buried
in the backyard, scent appearing on wet nights
like the pain in my left thumb. Instead a specific
tenderness for another animal, drawn by a child,
fangs melded into cheekbones, cutaway heart
in his three-fingered hand. Monster name, the year,
scribbled on the back, untraceable mix of capital
and lowercase trailing off the page.

Perhaps tomorrow I'll remember
the name of the monument to the stars,
city with the stairs, world's most famous
blue-roofed mosque, not this
endless string of numbers, confirmation
that I've paid, free like the internet
screens that open to me: baseless mountain
of sand, tiger sleeping in the sun.

The Poem

for Dunya

There was a poem I started, it had one good leg.
The one that seemed to want to run,
the one that had no shoes.

The poem that went its own way and never came back.

The poem I lost and the one that resurfaced
between breaths, in the grounds of my coffee.

The poem he wanted me to write—or she, or they. The one
that everyone hated and kept at a distance.

There was the poem that came disguised as spam,
the one that got stuck in my teeth,
and no one bothered to tell me.

The poem I scraped
like burnt toast into the trash.

There was the poem that sounded
like a bed hitting the wall, the one
everyone thought was something else.

There was the poem with too many tropes,
the one that danced for the wrong audience,
that expired before we could drink it.

There was the one that needed birds
or something wet to finish it,
the one I ate with the smallest spoon.

There was the poem my friend told me
was waiting for me. I saw it in the window,
slowly lifted my hand to wave,
but the light changed
and one of us looked away.

Three Poems

after Terry Winters's paintings

i. Tracer

I split

I freefell

separable

made you

follow

your focus

the problem

cellular

I let go

proved to be

like a bullet

smoke or dye

the stray

divided

detectable

pattern

        identified

ii. Aggregation

I cling to you
like a pod
      my pod, who will
      join us
there are many
attached as
      a burr to another
      and then
          so many more
          and then
enough
      we can stay
      like this until
forever then?

iii. Schema (25)

       put

fingers in
       its holes

             hang it
from a tree

       like a hornet's
nest   only blue,

       so

          blue

       what

I made of

       my desire

empty

       buzz

            easily
moved
       by sound
          scape

pardons

            paper-thin

How to Name the Baby

Straddle the puddle, one foot in mud,
the other dry. Storm a crowd of crows,
drop a stick down a stream. Swirl
literary allusions into your conversations.
Savor a trickle of vodka, an answer
to your constant thirst. Weave a mat,
then give it to the doctor with eyes
like your father's. Carry his surprise
like a smell on your clothes.
Turn coffee grounds over swiftly
on a lace tablecloth. Study the mess
until you find an endangered animal.
Measure the circumference
of your mother's waist, the night
she was married. Tell everyone
it came to you in an instant:
simple, easy, though regrettably,
hard to pronounce.

Fiction

My daughter shrugs lies like spring jackets—
left on a merry-go-round, caught in the branches
they fall from her lips colorful, half-forgotten:
we have a French bulldog from a breeder out west,
just eight weeks old and already trained.
At first I'd stretch, too, pat its head every morning.
A squeal, a gentle shove out the back door—all a fiction.
Of course, I'd falter at times, trip up with her friends
old enough to sniff out the feigned antics, our empty laps.
Stories taking shape like pearls between our uneven jaws.
A rare barker among the breed. We had to send her back.
Here's the heart-shaped metal tag bearing her name,
there, the fenced yard where she ran a worry path
between the red and yellow daffodils,
the freshly sprouted weeds.

All Guesses Are Wrong

*after Margaret Wise Brown**

Dear Gertrude,

For attending to my request—
thanks my only one, surrealist
no men at dusky desks, hearts askew, just
your book for young minds
no comma. Love the dog and the girl
Rose and Rose and bite now the sweet boat,
white capped, frosting the sea
that like me doesn't sleep
(always the will to be).
I once owned their upturned eyes
like lemonade downed between
cubes of ice, wrought iron chairs
sifting through fountains of salt,
columns of feet atop shoulders,
purple shadows, late afternoon mix.
Waxing or waning, why ask me?
It's about the view from here, not the moon
but the mouse, old lady, broom, room,
the dog sailing the world is round
and round it goes. I stopped living
when I stopped kicking. My wonderful house
above the sea, melting into what's left
of the cake. I've been touched.
Good night now, sweet dreams.

---

* In 1938, Margaret Wise Brown sent letters to eminent writers of the day including John Steinbeck, Ernest Hemingway, and Gertrude Stein asking them to write children's books for a series she edited. Stein was the only one to respond. *The World Is Round* was published in 1939.

Love Letter to A

Abandon alliteration, for the heartbeat, pause, hum under you, A,
frame pending art, arbitrary as nature, amber alert of sudden petals,
what creates this shade but
our heads
pressed
together
in
pain?
That
night you
escaped,
I called,
you came
without
glancing
back.
A
language
absent
ardor. I
lean instead on
the leap, inevitable swallow, your patter, patois. Magic in the
unexpected arrival, *abracadabra*, absent you, death's silent partner,
there's nowhere to aim.

Sister

for Janine

She was less than two
when she crawled to the back of a closet,
ate mothballs that lined a suitcase,
savored them like butter mints,
naphthalene-tinged, hoping one might
taste better than the last. My sister
who they waited months to name, lost parents
not expecting the fifth final child.
She emerged, mouth open, fragrant
breath a simmer. Our father unleashed
his fear down the hall. *She's dead,*
dead for sure. Left our mother
to discover for herself the distinct
scent, our sister's paling face.

Every mother secretly has a favorite child
born in moments like these. Ours traded saviors
for action, syrup of ipecac and sirens,
a rush of feet down the carpeted stairs.
Her whispered prayer: a saving newly named
christened, awake, home the next day.
Their marriage unraveled on the curb—
too quick to collapse in presumed defeat.
And that smell of something preserved
or old, tucked away, makes me think of my sister
still tough, unnamable to this day.
Her sighs heavy next to mine
emanating murmurs of wool coats steam-cleaned
double patched elbows, sweet sweat of breath.

Tangent

In the painting the woman is surrounded by oranges. Bright green background and then oranges ad infinitum. Some sprout from trees, others pop seemingly from midair. And her in the foreground a veil just below her eyes, sloping up at the corners. A low-cut dress, round breasts, perfect circles.

My husband says, *just remember the lathe makes a circle.* He winds the wheel forward, stops, winds it back. He wants me to be inspired by machines. At night he dreams my silver bracelets float from my wrist each one now separate and silent. *The lathe makes a circle,* I repeat as I walk to work, do dishes, fall asleep.

The circle is nature. Shape of tree rings. Dead center of every flower. Place to start a story. Round robin in the classroom, cross-legged on the floor. Whoever isn't with us, please join the circle now.

We call it *the one with the seven eyes.* It hangs on the wall, faded turquoise ceramic. A circle in the middle surrounded by six smaller ones. Above the baby's crib, the entrance to a home. Protect us from the envy of others' eyes.

There was a night my father saw the moon in my eyes, slipped the perfect paper ring around my too skinny finger, orange glow of the cigar fading in and out as we walked.

My mother studied the lens of the eye under an electron microscope. Magnified each thin layer. A cross section. Pupil, retina, cornea, sclera. She said even the universe is curvilinear. Movement of a ball or bullet through space.

Today my father is sitting on his balcony peeling an orange, he twists his hand toward the sun, careful not to let the juice drip below his wrist. Soon he will lose his left eye. Cancer floats in first, then the knife. And we will live our days as if under a bell. The silent curve of walls. Wait for the tap, the vibrations to begin.

Alleyway

Ghazal

Spring never came easily to me anyway,
I hate the bite of green, sudden scent along the pathway.

All season I remain uninterested in its fragrant smolder,
its disregard for sofas and standing half-asleep in doorways.

The continual expression of abundance wears on me
broadcasting vigor in an everyday *just love me kind of way*—

small burst of blinding purple or yellow and misty-eyed,
I know all the names both Latin and otherwise

before they fall from gardener's tongue, here's my Solomon's
seal, hollyhock, wild rose, blooming, even in the alleyway.

Cakewalk, Detroit 1976

Cakewalk's history, hidden in another room or absent.	For sale signs like teeth on every street, new ones each dawn.	Like a sonnet a cake leans into the box it's in, our arms around it.
Suburban schools, Catholic schools step over meaning.		Sonnet's a walk too. Pause, turn, move again retrace lines.
Walking home with my sister, a box. I thought he wanted what I'd won.		My aunt never said crazy she said touched, as in Were you? Was she?
Hands outstretched. Boys touch, no questions. I didn't know.		Then my mom was a box of light, my dad a box on the move, a window seat.
I wanted to reach my hand into tree, cloud, pot ready to boil.		A week later the city was covered in ice. Every street, a long slide.
Bring back the flock, family corner home, the fort we once made of cold.	You can tell a lot about someone by the way they carry a box. Leave.	The breaking of branches a song too, the melt the salt, its own price.

What to Count

What does it mean to hold your mouth to another's ear. What does it mean to make something stealth. Where do you feel it. Where do things happen when they happen on a train.

A shelter that falls in on itself. A hospital that can't help you, a pencil without lead. Are there things you could use.

A whisper what does it excite in you. She said stand on the corner with a sign should I? Something falling soft in the air tiny disappear your skin damage with a capsule. It is a good way to eat all the time. He doesn't want the numbers in the bag—100.150.200.250.300. Women, children, the old only.

What matters is that you are innocent when you die like this.

Step into the flash. Remember this day. Don't throw rice for the birds, a bubble you catch in your teeth. Smile's not right. The scent behind your ear makes his head hurt.

Sent home crying when the visitors came through hands in pockets and chewing gum and pencils and penicillin and taking notes. Bombs dropped last week didn't they? In the schoolyard. Where are your dual-use shoes.

What counts is the circle when you dance like this.

Up out of the water too much chlorine in the backyard pool, see it in their eyes. Children. Looking into the sun. What is on the other side.

They say we can't fill the order not even one drop on a hot stone. Nothing will be clean or white again. The x-ray of your wrist, chest, lungs will be done by hand, come back in seven hours. There are too many young men they will die of general malaise right in the street and there is one ambulance in the city and there is nowhere for it to take you.

What counts when you fall like this is the way they lift you bending at the knees.

II

Persistence

Arch Action

There's a problem the rain is calling us to solve
perfect structure, a band of leaves dismantled and
falling

A solution a thousand years in the making
internal ties or external bracing, curve of bricks
mirrored in the pond

There's the hold you feel, the echo your feet make
under its shape, dull in the earth something speaks back
a pulling

a boy once told me it's my shadow that's straight not me
released from any constraint my arms have a life of their own
begin floating

Love

The endless beeping of my daughter's alarm this morning woke me but nobody else. I remember someone telling me that it's the teen years when you lose the most sleep, not when they are babies. And today I know it's true. Now I follow her movements around the park with a boy. She's a small black dot on my phone. He's beside her, I know, even though I don't see him. I imagine him as a shadow circle beside hers. His parents don't know they are together, don't approve. It occurs to me that first love is often disrupted by someone, by friends, by parents, or siblings. They step into that glowing circle, try to interrupt the bloom. But what is love if not persistence?

I imagine they stop to sit on a bench, walk hand in hand, catch glimpses of fish from the bridge over the pond. I wonder if she tells him about her birthday party near that same pond where we looked for bats years ago. Their houses tall on top of poles. A gaggle of girls in the dark tromping through wet grass. We had a tool to help us monitor the bats' movements. Above our heads they moved away from the static of us, uninterested in being found, like she is suddenly silent in my hand. When she was born, she held my gaze so intently, I lost my own breath, could only match hers.

When I'm nervous, I feel my pulse in my palms, an echo of my heartbeat or hers. I have a long-held habit of knocking on wood that's persisted for many years. I knock on door frames and windowsills, headboards and end tables. Sometimes it's to drive away that unnatural sound. They say the concept evolved in Scandinavian countries; the knocking meant to release hidden tree fairies. I do it most often to bring someone home safely.

The man who tried to teach me to speak Arabic when I was younger than my daughter is now shares a name with her love, the most popular boy's name the world over. He was a teenager, my second cousin. He came dutifully to our home in Baghdad out of respect for my father. His singular focus never seemed to wane, even when I screamed as I heard him arrive, hid under tables, pretended to be sick.

After we left, he married and had a family. He became a schoolteacher and later a principal. My father joked with him about choosing this path after teaching me, but I saw it in him even then: persistence in the face of daily obstacles. He was killed in front of his home, gunned down when he answered the door, among the many educators, scientists, and academics killed that year and that have continued to be since. His family left on the other side, missing his return.

Truth

for Amin

Take the meekest mean street in Detroit to the closest patch of commerce available in 1978 and you will find a pancake house. All sticky surfaces and silverware falling from tables to floor, fork against knife, and the up and down din of conversations. Look for the boy who was widely believed to be named for the dictator. Sit close to him, close enough to smell the syrup licked from the corner of his mouth. Notice his exuberance can't be contained by the white plastic chair, reminiscent of a tulip. Know that there was only one instruction his mother gave as she helped him out the door: *Don't tell your father I had you baptized.*

His father had just returned from a year in Iraq where he'd been tasked with helping encourage back the academic class, doctors and scientists who'd left the country over the past decade. Now he is back and craving pancakes and family. He'd left them in Detroit to fend for themselves in abandoned schools, then Catholic schools, where nothing made sense, not the words or the gestures. But to say the boy is angelic is also true—small for his age, rosy cheeks, blond ringlet curls and green eyes. Understand the boy knows little of religion. He doesn't yet know his family is a direct descendent of the prophet or that his great-great-great-grandfather wrote an often studied and analyzed exegesis of the Koran. This lacuna in the boy's knowledge would overflow several water glasses and it was somebody's fault, not his own.

The boy has been trying to get a word in for some time. See how he's not taken a bite from his stack in several minutes. His mother's words have faded and become confused with his desire to capture his father, turn attention away from his siblings, toward him. See him suddenly waving his napkin above his plate, as if he's going to perform a trick, make something disappear. Know the confession poised on his lips.

Art

beautiful Iraqi girl never appeared in a book before then. she was in a poem. the man who wrote her was a famous poet, and before that, a journalist. his poems looked like boxes. justified. all the words pooled around her that first time.

beautiful Iraqi girl became my shadow. she was more dedicated to her family than i was back then. i was passing through, always on my way to someplace else. nights on the floor, or when lucky, tucked into the guest beds in friends' houses. in the afternoon, tired of waiting for busses, i'd walk to the next stop, throw away my transfer. i left school before it ended. i disappointed my family up close. they wondered what i was looking for, anyways. I found her in the main library. she stuck out to me, like a gap-toothed smile. a sign of royalty.

for a while, I talked about the poem to men at parties, felt it under my shirt when I walked away from them. it was written before the first. *desert storm.* I never wanted to emulate it. my hands became other sparer poems. about the day-to-day. war. not a sudden tragedy that brings you close to someone you'd never sit next to otherwise.

something tragic happened to *her*. a family member murdered. that's why he entered the house. sat next to her on the couch, noticed her beauty. he did not comment on the food. its smell or the offering of it. never mentioned religion. he was there to cover a story. I do not know if he asked after anyone else. what became of the *w*'s, the *h*'s, the *a*'s in his story. he moved on. won awards for his poems. maybe he forgot her. that poem no one asks after anymore. it's so long ago now.

What Every Driver Must Know

If it was good enough for Baltimore, it was good enough for Baghdad.

Upon completing a new traffic code for Iraq modeled after the state of Maryland's.
Imperial Life in the Emerald City, Rajiv Chandrasekaran

More phantom hands in this dying city
now leaving blue booklets
tucked under our windshields.
Traffic instructions so worthless
King Hammurabi won't even lift a finger
to breathe meaning into these laws.

light reflective clothing should be worn
when walking during darkness or
cloudy weather, hold the steering wheel
with both hands, for every hour driven,
rest for five, learn to yield, to wait

We drive old Toyotas, clothesline holding
the doors closed, "Seven Eyes" muted turquoise
dangling from rearview to protect us from evil
eyes, as if anyone could find someone left
to envy here.

The courtesy at a four-way stop,
white-gloved traffic police
with ten confiscated cars and pockets full of dinars.
Checkpoints, IEDs, decisions to make
every time we venture out in a car,
speed or stop, flee or comply.

The potential to bleed, we all have it—
to explode in a market, soccer game
among friends, in lines waiting
for a job or news of the missing.
We carry our dead the way ants do,
dragging corpses with intensity and care.

There are many to bury
before the sun goes down.

While you speed to reach beyond the barricades,
cool greenness of safety enlightened
occupiers. Dusk the most dangerous time
to drive, except here. Suburban GMCs, Hum-
vees, obey the speed limit set
35 miles per hour.

the driver must be seated, focus on the task
at hand, keep from staring at any one object
for too long, avert your eyes from the sun

From our arak-soaked dreams some Valium
cloudy mornings, we speak of leaving.
Measure the miles with pebbles, dropped teeth,
bones, burnt clothing, scarves.
Leave you to embed your limbs in our cars
streets, homes, when we have all
gone, pushing through doorways, exit
map in hand.

Roadside shells of cars line the highways
burnt then whitewashed by the sun,
brought to life by the wind only,
passing vehicles.

The trees will greet you then,
the ones that grow here and
no place else on earth.
Remember the taste for me
of the fruit, sweet then bitter,
and the small petals falling
white in the yards.

Capture the Flag

In this game we try to burn down the house
cooking foreign foods on a holiday no one knows
to celebrate. We fumble our way into the bedroom—
glass doorknob lost, screwdriver in hand—and sleep
curled in one bed holding forth with the overseas
operator. Each word is an echo punctuated
by beeps, seconds ticking into years of missing
family. We come from nowhere, from Cleveland,
from Baghdad named for dictators and distant relatives
like shady garden patches full of uneatable vegetables,
frying pans still smoldering in a snowbank,
round Iraqi sausages charred on a paper napkin.

We came to Detroit for a funeral and never left
the all-electric house, ivy smothering bricks, birds nesting
in chimneys. Perched ourselves on a tree
that didn't grow up but out. Ran the streets,
feet tagging the center island, safe. Games named
for actions never realized: capture the flag, ghost
in the graveyard, Marco Polo. The object always to appear
normal, American, unafraid, fast as doors slamming,
borders closing, between us and them, language
peppered with the wrong words, customs that dissuaded
friendships beyond the front porch, flight path
forming above roof lines, even as it disappeared.

Burnished in Future Time

after Abdel Hadi Al Gazzar's
Two People in Space Outfits

some say we came from nowhere
traveled beside meteors
a light between dark matter

the occupiers followed too, close
on our tails
always

their tongues and hands laden
with copper pots, a replica
of the first lock and key,
bitter oranges

unafraid of cosmic dust
mouths opened in
song

long ago the first recipe
was carved in earth, now plucked bare:
stuffed pigeon in clay pot

whose ingenuity will be lifted
through the narrowing window,
author, museum, thief, or bird?

Uprising

Why is there confusion always
about the size of the crowd,
the number of dead,
the exact time
the war or revolution began?

Gathered on bridges,
standing in squares,
clouded in tear gas
scarves pressed to mouths
emptied canisters thrown
into a mass of bodies,
the bloody on makeshift stretchers,
crowd opening for one,
then the next, the next.

Everything's been makeshift
for so long: cars and careers,
hospitals and plans.

Days of no lights, no jobs,
no school, turned into
months, breaks in the wars,
blockades, as hard to count
as the flour in the bag, gas
in the car, fruit on the trees
in the orchard, only a memory.

They try to pull the blinds down
so no one can see us like this
rising from morning until night,
shut down communication as if
these shouts, the crowds,
wouldn't find their way
to someone with pen and paper
to document again,
if nothing else, again.

The next morning dead birds
organized like martyrs
along the edges of the flag
the photo shared
ten thousand times over.

What is left to carry
a nation of people toward
the bridge again today
except that anticipation,
thick in the air. A new country,
like birds black and rising
above their shoulders.

Detroit 1998, a reminiscence

after Eliot Weinberger

In Detroit there is no fresh fruit.

We eat with our eyes. Our children are strong as weeds. They learn the alphabet backwards and grow up never wanting to leave.

Our streets are named for cigarettes highways—winning lotto numbers.

In Detroit we don't stop at stop signs and traffic lights never turn red.

We crave the smell of gasoline.

There exists only one map of the city. The mayor keeps it facing the wall in his home and you must pay a fee to look at it.

The casino coughs blood into the night sky and the incinerator wears a surgical mask.

In Detroit our smiles are crooked, our canine teeth sharp as diamonds or hard candy sucked to a fine point.

When it rains the streets smell like tortillas and wine and we play games where you must gather with only those who look exactly like you.

In Detroit vines grow out the doors and windows of the oldest churches and you must cross the street or travel with a machete to pass them.

There are seven kinds of birds that gather by railroad tracks at noon and dusk. All the gardeners in the city take turns watching over them.

In Detroit our factories sleep with one eye open, their histories written in code on internal walls.

All our cats are feral. They live on the roofs of our public buildings. Packs of dogs have been sent to unseat them.

For in Detroit there is a secret freeway with only one car, its headlights dimmed, and the sound of its bass makes roadside flowers grow.

The river is full of socks, hijabs, bicycle tires. Old men fish for hours off the sinking pier.

In Detroit we cover our houses with fine mesh and ivy. Wild roses grow everywhere.

Slow Work

I'm almost done with my career
as a worrier, they say think
about a giant tortoise
oldest living land mammal
walking with a rose between
its tired teeth, now just try
to replace that picture
with any other, its hard
shell, lumbering walk
one foot dragging a bit
marking its path in the sand.
I see nothing now but you
coming toward me, glory
or no glory, work's just
the same.

Bite It

like every loose nail
bit of lip, torn cheek
until you see stars
faint and dancing

like a short pencil
familiar as your teeth
the ones you dream of losing,
tongue searching for comfort
in that bloodless hole

like dogs can't smell cancer cells,
pawing at skin, like sand
never gives way under us,
like everything, aspirin
or apple isn't coated
with a bit of death

bite it like the ear
from another poem,
fraught with meaning,
a grape you saved for last,
for the way it held
its perfect shape.

Grief

I climb peaks and dips
assemble myself below your awning
this night the sky filled star—one
corner pinned back I
hang on your sigh, the paused
way you say my name
solitary half-swallow
before your voice disappears
and there are only your eyes
silent "don't forgets"
the teasing out
one constellation from an
other to say this brightness
might hide the facts of your death
makes my aloneness as irrelevant now
as the thousand calls to prayer
before your last painless shrug
all the trembling lights that ceased
their shining years ago.

III

Portrait

Skip

a palindrome after Nate Marshall
for Bridget Wolff
September 1965–February 2019

I'll buy your daughter a leopard
print scarf. By then you'll be dead.
Your voice, a squeak, the sound

a pack of wolves makes before they howl,
a broken elevator trying to contain its freefall.
The thought of you then makes me want

to walk backward up a flight of stairs
or down a tree-lined street. You were filler-
paper notes and exaggerated promises.

You didn't know you had a spot in your brain
where the lies sprouted. I'll be right back,
you said. You disappeared for twenty years.

You are thirty-seven years from your death in drama
class, fairy tale characters switch roles, villains
suddenly good, the innocent, tinged with evil.

You were goldilocks, already
had the hair, red cape, lipstick, shoes.
He almost gave up his groping for the part.

Lumbering with a briefcase, man-boy-wolf,
the class howled when the teacher called
your name. They didn't know
even two can be a pack.

We walk in the door, sign in,
leave again, a six-story monolith

down the street from Motown Records.
Our days a long skip, a ghost ride
down the corridor of the city.

Tab cola, one sip left, your mouth,
the bottle, wiped clean of its red stain.
Your kiss on a pile of notes, I'll keep

forever. 1982 and the sun sets then rises
pink as dippity-do. On Belle Isle still
at noon. We should be in school.

Self-Portrait as Vacuum

after Tarfia Faizullah

All first thoughts are domestic
then vintage, model number
canister or stand up straight
       intake the long
       breath,
dirt.
rote
movements
patterned
like the sun's
rays,
bypass
the far
corner, ants.
let every
thing
tremble and
go. small
splinters
of gold
and red
glass,
pale leaves
of the
failing
money
tree,
nearly
swallowed
orange
seeds,
a twice
folded
note

to myself,
send out
the poems.
strands
of our hair
now one tight circle.
release the cord, track the knocking sound:
small bottle of pale pink nail polish hung up
somewhere, which one was it, *Baby's Breath,*

                           Whispered Lore,

                                    Barely There?

Medusa Cement

She took
what I said
out of context
she took
what I said
and put it
in her hair
her hair
which spiraled
to the floor
or on occasion
floated to the ceiling.

She took
what I said
and ground it up
really small
it was some words
she put them
into the building
I mean when
the building
was built
facing the water
my words were
mixed in.

Trumbull Song

Once a girl was
from land of Trumbull
and tree-named streets
but more than
the name
the place she flies above
at night and in dreams.

She sees the field
on corner, once a house
were right there
Sam the Tailor
locked up, Sharky's dark
pay phone hanging
the apartment on Butternut
all its bricks stolen
and no roof.

She goes over the store now
Norm's Liquor Express
sees a deer there
smelling garbage, the air,
across the street
the church all gargoyled
and black, like fire
once touched parts
of its outside.

Like the deer were too,
had escaped from another place
time to breathe again, and run fast
or fly above like on a carpet
knees tucked underneath.

But tomorrow in the morning
when she rides by
the deer is gone
she stares there
from the window
and wishes it safe
back in a field or a forest.

Because it is the names
that might fool you
Pine, Sycamore, Spruce
Elm, Ash
and the stillness of almost daylight
that could get you lost
make you crazy
fly in circles
like garbage
or slow, like a tumbleweed
down deserted Trumbull Ave.
and she above it
can see it
fix it all up
from her dream
from the air.

It is the stillness she takes with her
when daytime does come
and the distance is different
from the ground,
she remembers
all her nights
and is calm
as she walks now
home from school
streets and blocks.

She finds a picture
in her mind
of every different tree
shape of leaves
and she wants the deer back
to walk with her
these now tree-lined
streets.

Back to School

in memory of Nasir

I went back to school to learn
all the things hands could hold
zippers pulled closed,
paper unfolded and refolded
the lines dotted or unbroken, dark
scissors that leave marks
erasers held tight.

I went back to feel the pressure
spinning in circles, arms at sides, then
flat on the grass, book bag on chest
clouds beyond a wooden frame,
the worry, a structure held firmly in place.

I went back because I didn't understand
civics, revision, how to manage
time, stop the collapse of economies
or bees raiding each other's hives
queens toppled in the dark.

I went back to school to find a boy
his unassigned stories, parallel fantasies
friends as characters with new animal names
at recess he greets them as Goat-Man
ready to scale the playscape, his menagerie
lined up close behind.

A mother drives so many times over her fear,
to the place and back again.
This boy's mother no longer knows that highway
in remotely the same way as you or I,
grief bundled or coming loose
in the backseat nothing strapped
or humming, no stories unfolding
out the window, animals hiding in the trees.

Lynndie's Other Voice*

An ancient symbol,
eye in the palm, hypnotizing
from a *Three Stooges* rerun—
what I knew of these parts
before I arrived to a prison,
already bad history
behind its walls.

All the men's eyes looked the same,
black and dull as the dogs they feared.
There "some things stay in the house"
meant a secret, not an animal,
a leash we kept on the wall
camera-ready.

How does a bad idea keep going—
you know something, see
something, a knife out of a drawer
on the wrong night,
matches near bone-dry trees.

Tolerance had little room. We were all just bodies,
some on top, some on bottom.
We called it training. The fence was invisible,
guidelines never give. Torture pure
not simple. You could have asked me
what day it was, who my friends were,
I didn't know. They were all the same,
until they weren't.

---

*   Lt. Lynndie England was six months pregnant at the time of sentencing for her role in the torture of Iraqi prisoners at Abu Ghraib.

It's hard for you to believe,
I'm not the woman you saw
doing those things. She is the dirt
I was born into, but not the fruit
from my tree.

When I have my child,
I will not name him
in regret or sorrow, from false love or
secrets held. I will call him
for the miracle he is
to have come from this
nothing else.

Mayfly

for Esmé

You have the right
to be delicate, transparent

yet still
flatten yourself against
the strong current

appear as if you're caught
in mid-swarm
when you are singularly

flying toward the light.

Mess

A poem is built of bricks
of chocolate, nuts like white
stars. My teeth long
to find the soft bit
of dried fruit
the sour
dazzle.

Mouth me the words, poet,
or motion to me, discreet
like a passing window
to clean the dark
mess with my
tongue, open
sleeve.

Lipstick

1. Cherries in the Snow

Imagine the snow like
sand it stings
your teeth when
you bite something soft
and it is really hard
to catch blood
dripping from your chin.

2. Crushed Candy

Honeysuckle pinched
ding-dong ditch
neighbor's handprints
ring the small one's neck.

3. Eternal Petal

Every part
of the circle
needs one
move your hand
or the paper
as you go.

Hiding

It was no ordinary moon, but a super moon glowing above and between houses. They were running in its cool white light. The mother was running from her daughter. Was she sixteen or seventeen? First she was the one chasing, then she was the chased. One of them went to stare at the moon. Not together. Not tonight. One chin lifted, one set of shoulders hunched. One bathrobe coming loose.

It was not a warm night in the conventional sense, but warm for early December. Both the mother and her daughter were out of shape. The daughter had some height on her and could see above tall bushes and fences. For a time, she trained as a ballerina and still had moments of grace, lifting her long neck, arms moving in unison as she pressed back the branches behind the garage.

The mother stood behind the tree in the backyard like a large garden statue. Occasionally she leaned out to watch for her daughter, hands shielding her eyes from the glare. The tree towered over the deck near the crab-shaped red sandbox where the daughter used to play. It stayed uncovered, no matter the weather. The daughter never played with dolls in the house, but there were those she left in the sandbox seasons on end. Long blond hair, yellowy and plastic, covered in sand and earwigs. Later she'd rounded a bend. Started liking pink.

She could hear her daughter humming from a distance. It was a popular song about a former stripper who became rich. The verse she remembered was about buying her mom a new car. Maybe motherhood lives in the gesture reciprocated, good or bad, she thought. Maybe my day will come.

Earlier in the week, the mother had read about the sound the earth makes deep at its core. Scientists described it as a bell, constantly ringing. She felt sure that it shivered up her spine as she stepped away from the tree, out of hiding.

Six Poems

for Ann Mikolowski

(1) Photo

wash the photo
with a damp cloth
you say they always
look at me like
I am their mother
I want another picture
sneak up on them
wipe that look away

(2) Windowsill

bend Olive Oyl's long
legs into the small egg-
colored convertible
she is planning a
trip to see her honey see
she will stop
to pick flowers
on her way

(3) Book

there is a rubber chicken
and a fat smiling cigar
in his mouth moon
shaving cream pie for
your face doggy drool
and hair stew
this is not dinner is
mashed potato leeks
ginger carrot salad
with flowers salmon

and wine banana cream
pie no one move
in the small dining room
it is all here happy
keep this night
names copied
later in the book
and the menu too

(4) Drawer

when a child comes open
for you spin hold hostage
lots of stuff (maybe even some
moved from the sill)
Lisa Simpson night-light
slime in a jar
cow magnet windup
chick trick cards
magic teeth place hand
and eye move fat
and fast oooohh
what to choose

(5) Painting

maybe they first
appear to you
like a magic lantern
vision out the kitchen
window three ladies
in odd Victorian hats
sailing a canoe between
houses into your
backyard they say
this is lush but
not quite home

they come round to
the front lift their
heavy skirts to find
your old address climb
the porch come in
join you on the couch
for a welcome rest

(6) You

you hold that big bunch of red flowers
close to your chest
open noon
island road
no car
no rush
just you thick
hair and smile
like stillness
caught you
this time
shoulders up
from the sun
voice out
near the ocean
breeze like
you talk

hey you
so good to see you
I have stories for you.

Carried Away

This is a portal into a first fight
windowpane view, later an embrace
mind still full of the spat, this flat where
a bike leans casually in the face of
thievery. Her growing wakefulness says:
trust in questions, emphasize agreement
between verb and noun, unless
something is just plain pursuit and
not worth pursuing. His answer: let's ride
that pony as long as we can make our margins.
Without questions how many times
can I give you the gist?
The rule is never jump to conclusions.
The truth is happening in the dark
cover of the photo, a stranger
pulls over, smiles idly, offers her a lift.

Poetry

Were you inspired by myth, religious texts, redacted promises
from the *Elements of Style*? Was there a view from your window
triangle of blue between thick branches?

Did you squeeze your eyes closed until colors transformed
into birds of prey? Open the book to a specific page,
circle every seventh word?

Was there an impediment of your own creation, a pain
below your heart, a way you chose not to breathe, a rock
you put between your toes?

Anecdotally, could you say it was a miracle,
the way the words washed over you,
bathing your face in light?

Circadian

doorway
into sleep
melts beneath
my tongue
faceless lullaby
pushes me
into the rhythm
my body lost

until a sound
in the walls
wakes me
and I wonder
whose imprint
left me behind
in the dark,
whose edges
didn't I touch?

sister whisper

a note behind her back
smudged red kiss folded inside
her lips married another
love's last night sinking
into the sand. mistaking him,
for her friendship
upending the summer.
painted fingernails match
chipped paint of the boat's bow
red falling off, revealing
white underneath.
inside, scaffolding and drop cloths
walls half poppy bright,
single flower in a coffee can
vase, she says:

we did everything you wanted to do
and you're still not my friend

Luck

Once I held that small bit
of my mother's dress,
blue like how the sky is
near the water
or in our dreams,
competing with itself always.
Now I wait center stage
in the lottery window
caught between
what was left
and what is here now.
Behind my small door
I hear your birthdays
and death days, visions
and repeating patterns,
license plate, old phone number,
perfectly even total
of the restaurant bill.
Circle the numbers,
call them out,
or let me choose.
Some people play once,
win once.

What ten questions can do for your community

Ten questions can carry a camera phone, a small knife, a handful of change through courthouse metal detectors.

Ten questions makes jokes to lighten the mood in long lines of poor people with problems. He can chew gum and look like any other man chewing gum.

He walks unafraid though he isn't from these parts. He surveys your roof shingles and reaches a hand into your mailbox.

Ten questions will tell your neighbors he is servicing your phone.

He buys his shoes where the policemen buy theirs, black and shiny. Studies himself wearing mirrored sunglasses reflected back in the tiny pupil of your eyes. He comes to meetings even though no one remembers inviting him. He's always the first or last to leave.

Ten questions can drive your car right out of your driveway. His ghost hands, clean fingernails, empty pockets.

He can smell the animal in your basement. He knew it was there before you did. He won't help you get it out.

Up north

for Suzi

tiny fish blanket the water's surface
a pickup truck runs us off the back road
taking picture of the full moon
on our phones

the moon runs us off the road
a pickup truck surfaces taking pictures of us,
fish beneath a blanket in back
full of water tiny, still

The Ocularist

The man bent over the new eye, drew its capillaries.
He graduated from art school but seemed normal.

Collared shirt, task lamp, face round and serious
as my father's. He knew I dated artists,

but the room was small, and there was no time for that dance.
He shook his pen, made it rattle.

I thought of a snake curled in a shoe.
As a child, we differed on what was normal.

I wanted to play outside; my father called it
running the streets. I imagine myself then, winged,

a knotty-haired girl, swift, limbs and clothes loose.
Ayuni, he'd beg on his gentler days, shaking his head.

I'd pretend I didn't see him, follow the shadows
that asked me to dance. The first days after surgery

my father could see through his eye's absence,
a swirl of colors. Once a famous writer told me

that's where she found poems—behind her
closed eyes visions waited like people exiting a train.

His, replaced by a black patch when he danced
at my brother's wedding. His last months, I tried

to make things seem normal, removed the eye
with a small suction cup, held it under water,

cleaned into its perfect curve. In its absence,
red and white streaks looked back at me.

We stopped spending time with the details.
The deep brown-black cornea, its fixed pupil.

Unless one studied hard, they wouldn't find its flaw:
it didn't move. I think of this person I met only once

like a still-life painting, among the glistening fruit,
the sliver of the everyday, their memory, an anomaly.

The small brick building on a busy road I drive by.
Imagine a man inside, a row of eyes before him to perfect.

The challenge unchanging as the palette
of grays, greens, brown, blacks, and blues.

How to match what's gone,
save the last bit of his art for the veins.

Self-Portrait at 56, (under the wire)

I guess I've found myself,
music paused, in the right square,
growing bit of flesh murmuring
above beltline, and ahh,
these lines down the center
of my face, eyes off kilter, they say
there's no symmetry in space, I relate
floating green earth. I want to melt
some days into a passing bus,
once in Prague I nearly died, felt
the wisp of the tram at my neck
so close my hair moved, daughter
and husband stunned on the far curb
amazing, really, how little I still notice
my surroundings most days
save the random, like a handprint
left on a wall, press me to say
what that wall means to me
and I can't.

Acknowledgments

"All Guesses Are Wrong": *We Call to the Eye and to the Night*, Persea Books

"Deadline": *the museum of americana: A Literary Review*

"Patterns of Departure": *Glue Gun*

"Lipstick": *Inclined to Speak: An Anthology of Contemporary Arab American Poetry*

"Lynndie's Other Voice": *Inclined to Speak: An Anthology of Contemporary Arab American Poetry*

"Mayfly": *Inclined to Speak: An Anthology of Contemporary Arab American Poetry*

"Medusa Cement": *Alternative Press*

"Pandemic": *The Detroit Free Press*

"The Poem": *Room Object*

"Self-Portrait as Vacuum": *Room Object*

"Six Poems": *Dispatch Detroit, Vol. 2*

"Tangent": *Malpaís Review* and *Brady Press*

"Trumbull Song": *Abandon Automobile*

"Truth": *Glue Gun*

"What Every Driver Must Know": *We Are Iraqis: Aesthetics and Politics in a Time of War*

"What to Count": *Dispatch Detroit, Vol. 2*

My unending gratitude to the following individuals and organizations for their support:

Suzanne Alousi-Miller, Amin Alousi, Janine Alousi, Hamid Alousi, Adrienne Alousi-Jones, Ismael Ahmed, Kazim Ali, Deborah al Najjar, Anan Ameri, Glen Armstrong, Terry Blackhawk, Hayan Charara, Sheila Esshaki, Cal Freeman, Jen Garfield, Lia Greenwell, Jennifer Hackett, Lolita Hernandez, Kim d. Hunter, M. L. Liebler, Joan Mandell, Peter Markus, Dunya Mikhail, Derek Miller, Marilyn Nelson, Kristin Palm, Pennacook Women, Kevin Rashid, Robin Reagler, Kathleen Schenk, and Carmen Yonan;

Arab American National Museum, Bear River, Fine Arts Work Center, Inside-Out Literary Arts colleagues and friends, Knight Arts Challenge Detroit, Kresge Arts in Detroit, Martha's Vineyard Institute of Creative Writing, Mesa Refuge, Soul Mountain, The Room Project, and Wayne State University Press;

and most of all, my loves: Klaus Berner and Esmé Berner.

About the Author

Alise Alousi is a 2019 Kresge Literary Arts Fellow and has received awards from Knight Arts Detroit, Mesa Refuge, and others. Her work has been widely anthologized including in the collections *To Light a Fire: 20 Years with the InsideOut Literary Arts Project*, *Abandon Automobile: Detroit City Poetry* (both Wayne State University Press), and *Inclined to Speak: An Anthology of Contemporary Arab American Poetry*. She works at InsideOut Literary Arts and has been an active part of the literary scene in metro Detroit for many years. She currently serves on the steering committee for Room Project, a workspace for women and nonbinary writers in Detroit, and teaches poetry to teens at the Arab American National Museum. She lives in Royal Oak, Michigan.